GIFTS

Poems for Parents

APRIL HICKOX   *Untitled*

Gifts

POEMS FOR PARENTS

Edited by

Rhea Tregebov

SUMACH
PRESS

NATIONAL LIBRARY OF CANADA
CATALOGUING IN PUBLICATION DATA

Main entry under title:
Gifts: poems for parents

ISBN 1-894549-15-5

1. Canadian poetry (English) — 20th century. 2. Parenting —
Poetry. I. Tregebov, Rhea, 1953 –
PS8287.P36G44 2002   C811'.54'0803520431   C2002-900860-3
PR9195.85.P27G44 2002

*Sumach Press acknowledges the support of
the Ontario Arts Council and The Canada Council for the Arts
for our publishing program.*

Printed and bound in Canada

Published by
SUMACH PRESS
1415 Bathurst Street, Suite 202
Toronto, Ontario Canada
M5R 3H8

www.sumachpress.com

For my son, Sasha Tregebov,
and my parents,
Sam and Jeanette Block.

CONTENTS

INTRODUCTION

The title of this anthology, *Gifts*, was taken from the poem of the same title by Kingston poet Bronwen Wallace, a writer whose fine poetry has inspired a generation of Canadian poets. The son in "Gifts" is miserable over the birthday gift he has bought for his mother. He is at that agonizing age — young enough to purchase the gift unthinkingly and old enough to soon realize it isn't quite right. The mother in the poem knows she is helpless to protect him from this small grief, and from so many larger griefs. He has given her this gift, this bittersweet offering; she has given him the flawed gift of life. We love fully and imperfectly.

Bronwen Wallace was one of the first poets I read who wrote of this parent-child dynamic with such honesty and clarity, who neither sugar-coated nor glossed over the experience of being a parent. This honesty and clarity was part of her project as a feminist writer; it was also part of who she was. Wallace wasn't about to erect artificial boundaries between the writing self and the self who was passionately committed to her child.

Wallace's work struck home, resonating with my own experience as a child, even though at that time I wasn't a parent myself. I also read Michael Ondaatje's "Bearhug" before I had any kids, and felt when I read it the same shock of recognition, the same sense that in this poem a truth had been mapped that hadn't been acknowledged before in literature. "Bearhug" takes on an apparently unremarkable daily ritual. The child's position as he waits, open-armed, for the goodnight kiss becomes an emblem of his absolute love and his absolute vulnerability. In this posture, this moment, the father in the poem recognizes his own terrifying responsibility to meet that love, as well as the understanding that his response will be, necessarily, human and imperfect: "How long was he standing there/ like that, before I came?"

Parents and children are indeed locked "like a magnet of blood" to one another. And this interdependence takes place within the nitty-gritty details of birthday presents and goodnight kisses. Such terrain has not, in the past, been the territory of Literature, because, like so much of domestic life, it has been invisible, or, if seen, considered unworthy. We need to make sense of our lives as parents.

We need to move beyond the gender stereotypes that idealize maternal love and ignore paternal love, beyond the Hallmark sentimentality or ridicule with which popular culture treats this love. When, as a parent, I have read those poems in which both the joys and sorrows of parenting were honestly portrayed, I have found a reflection of my own perceptions that feels more real than the greeting-card images of scrubbed, sunny, obedient children and flawlessly attentive parents. It's not as though I were absolved of my failings, my fears. But reading the poetry of others helped me navigate the perplexities, helped me to identify, if not to solve, the complexity of my emotions and to comprehend the blessing and terror of this most visceral of human experiences.

I think that as a poet, I began writing about being a parent not so much to correct misapprehensions or to vindicate my choices as to excavate my own terrors and pleasures. Because so much had been obscured and misrepresented before, particularly in the relationship between women and their children, I needed to create my own map, or at least add to the map-making that other poets had begun for me. Possibly a price is paid for our commitment to this subject matter; the taint of sentimentality and the stigma of triviality are still high. But it would have been impossible for me to have written otherwise, and I know that my life as a parent has had a profound and, I believe, a salutary influence on my writing.

We need these poems. We need the validation of what we've lived through. It has been heartening to see more and more writers take on this subject. And for me, it has been particularly heartening to read the work of male poets whose increased involvement with the upbringing of their children has allowed them to address their lives as fathers.

The poems in this anthology take us through the cycle of experiences and emotions that face parents, mothers and fathers, as their children's lives evolve — birth and those first moments of connection; the delight of first steps and the terror of those steps that lead our children away; the comfort we offer and the comfort we find; the puzzling transformation to maturity. These are poems that create a kaleidoscope of experience; their language reveals the spectrum of emotions that come with being a parent: the critical, the cynical, the joy, the wonder, the anger, the impatience. Yet all are underlined by the commitment to doing the best we can, to raising the child while at the same time caring for ourselves. Perhaps it is through the creative exercise and the creative journey of language that we have been able to retain our sense of self as we have raised our children. Together these poems form a human and intelligent chronicle of the remedial joys and difficult sorrows that being a parent entails. It is my hope that they will resonate with those new to parenting or those wearied by it, those contemplating taking on the part, and those who are reflecting upon their own roles as children.

Rhea Tregebov

March 2002

STEFAN

Stefan
aged eleven
looked at the baby and said
When he thinks it must be pure thought
because he hasn't any words yet
and we
proud parents
admiring friends
who had looked at the baby

looked at the baby again

P.K. Page

At The Horse Pavilion

We lost you once, at the Horse Pavilion,
on a day of snappy wind beating
five flags above that brilliant

nightmare green in the sun and beyond
prayer but ready to live on a diet of it
for the rest of our days, we ducked and ran

among faces made blank or tender by our terror,
so that we understood for the first time
that this was the way the world was

truly divided: into those faces that could be
startled into goodness, and those that could not,
but none of them worth anything at all to us

except for what they could tell us as we
kept calling out to them the only words left to us, *A little boy!*
and the colours of the clothes you were wearing,

while the polished horses
kept mindlessly clearing gates
that were hardships,

but distant, whitewashed,
the hardships of others,

and sounds mocked us too,
in that whinnied bright air, a ring of faint surf,
the civil, evil sounds of horsemen's applause,

and we ran into each other and ran back,
ran through the stadium of stalls and sick straw-smell

ran out into the sun
of the Pavilion's mud plaza and there you were,

on the other side of the soot track
that led towards the weeping green park,

your eyes fixed without flinching
on the main doorway, waiting for us to
come out sometime before dark and we fled to you,

crying your name and I could see in your eyes
how hard you'd been standing your ground against terror,
how long you'd been forbidding yourself to invent us,

as if in inventing us you'd have lost all
chance to see us come out to you,

but how brilliant you seemed, having
saved yourself from harm, you didn't know it,
you turned your face to the taut thigh of my skirt,

not to cry, and we walked that way,
my hand holding your head to me
while I could have sworn

I could feel you inhaling what I was thinking
through the skirt's grass-engraved cotton:
Until this moment I never knew what love is.

Elisabeth Harvor

ON THE BIRTH OF KATHERINE ANNE MARTIN

I called out to the long kitchen shadows stretching
    around behind the refrigerator, say,
    listen to this! Knock
off your Mr Fantastic routine, the
    world is changed, let's dance the *macareña*
    in Javanese, on the cupboards, I

threw open the windows to the
cold night — the stars were fixed, dilated,
    mesmerized, I
cried out — let's have a wink, or at least a twinkle
    down on the brand new child's cradle,
    or whatever they're calling the hospital version!

Downstairs I ran and told the brown spider
    on her web (and she sends
    her heartiest congratulations,
    having 730 thousand of her own) and the myriad
    dustmites too finite to fathom an event
    of such magnitude (not their fault, so am I).

My furnace and water-heater flames seemed
    flickeringly pleased at the news, swaying
    in their twin vestal chambers. Which

brings me, I guess, to my own response, which I
    can't for the life of me put into words.
    So I'll just light all the candles in the house
    and get more quick things
    dancing at the news.

Ken Howe

BIRTH

They said the first six weeks
would be the hardest   they said there would be
resentment and then the guilt
my wife would not love the child instantly
and both of us would run
I would be hemmed in like a
fighter going down for the last time
I would long for
a single night's sleep
the undisturbed dawn   a day away from
the stink of things   that much time
without the guilt
knowing exactly how long
I'd been away from home   how much
she needed me   my wife and the child thing
that bound me to her like pain   bound me
to so much of the world that could only mean
money and time   work and eat
They said it would happen that way
I would become an adult   birth
was part of that job
They smiled when they asked their questions
and those who had children of their own

they could wait   they could
wonder when I would finally
catch fire   would it take a year or maybe
ten?   And I remember too
what they said   it gets better

Better when the child
begins her own story   a smile
to start with   looking back at somewhere
inside your head and that's the signal
everything is going to be
all right   The day she learned there were rules in the world
she learned to duck coming out from under tables
making noises that sound like questions
filling in a space around us
we didn't know was there
After her bottle and her blanket   after
her mother there is me
big old man no longer afraid to tell a stranger
the tiny words of love   love and the need
to be charged again by something human
like the morning when her arms go up to me
Will she speak today   will the word
burn and glow   catch fire in my mind

empty it till there is nothing
but the sound of blood speaking to blood

She stands by the window
almost a year   It took me
twenty-nine years to reach this place beside her
They said this would be
such another place   I did not know
there were babies everywhere and mothers who can
hold us all together   There is something
familiar in me again that
makes me big   Now it is my turn to say
I understand   I have been inside that room
with the lights and the doctors when
she shimmers in the air like viscera
I hear her lungs explode as the blood
turns in its place and is home   look god look she is
alive like her father who stands up inside his eyes and is
delivered to the good world again

David Zieroth

OFFERING

I was alone with you after everyone was gone
and life was in you like a charge in a wire. Your poor
head in my hand, musketball heavy, your eyes roving
for purchase in the blue and grey room. They had you
in a tiny surplice, not knowing
they didn't have to make you look holy, you were
already ministering to me.

The world you came from was already fading, a cry
from another room. This one so rude to want
so much of you already. Who wouldn't cry for it
in your position? Instead, serene, you somehow
manage peaceful silence, saving up for the yaw
of life, its raw colour and noise. Carrying you in
through the garden, you seemed to fit between the rain.

When you open your mouth now, there's a pink
quiet there, a cradle for speaking to grow in. It pulses
sound inchoate. But no words
are needed yet, no names for things,
no answers, no prayers, despite your head,
which nods in supplication, your white
choirboy hospital gown. For now,

you are the only word and the mouths
of our bodies spoke it.

Michael Redhill

CHRISTINE MACK *Light and Shadows*

You Begin

You begin this way:
this is your hand,
this is your eye,
that is a fish, blue and flat
on the paper, almost
the shape of an eye.
This is your mouth, this is an O
or a moon, whichever
you like. This is yellow.

Outside the window
is the rain, green
because it is summer, and beyond that
the trees and then the world,
which is round and has only
the colours of these nine crayons.

This is the world, which is fuller
and more difficult to learn than I have said.
You are right to smudge it that way
with the red and then
the orange: the world burns.

Once you have learned these words
you will learn that there are more
words than you can ever learn.
The word *hand* floats above your hand
like a small cloud over a lake,
The word *hand* anchors
your hand to this table,
your hand is a warm stone
I hold between two words.

This is your hand, these are my hands, this is the world,
which is round but not flat and has more colours
than we can see.

It begins, it has an end,
this is what you will
come back to, this is your hand.

Margaret Atwood

MADAM ABUNDANCE

A pen and ink drawing might
begin with the head, the shoulders,
but this one could begin with a circle
and in that circle the lopsided eye
of the drowsed nipple

or when it's aroused or in use
that stubbed pink castle of flesh in its
pebbled moat of pigment, sturdy
schoolboy's eraser, sucked and gleaming
and hung in the milk-heavy
bag of the breast.

The baby, bee to flower,
blindly nosing its way to its
medicine dropper of milk,

and for the mother
the sting of the mouth her
firstborn bee

Attachments!
The string of drool connecting the
tiny white pill of the miniature cardigan's
single button to one of the six much more
pearly and womanly buttons

on the milk-dampened blouse of the breast,
this drooled string the sibling to a

drooped string of garden saliva
slung between flower and flower

(the taller, the smaller)

on a Monday that will be
a hot, humid Monday
morning in August.

But now
it's fogged sunrise,
hour of non sequitur:

memories of husband-breath
the night this baby may have been
begun — the husband bashful and
bowing in at the door
of the parlour with his

come-out-to-the-garden-to-play smile.
He is young, he is scrubbed but

erotic, his mouth cool
as ether but with mint in it,

the wife is lolled on the sofa
reading *War and Peace,* she is risen
warm as baked bread, she is half-brown
from the sun and her blouse three-quarters
undone, a drift of rose-petal pink, her eyes
demurely sly, their lids

such drooped and wanton
know-it-all flowers that when the
husband drops to one knee to take a nipple
into his mouth, his own eyes

closed with the pleasure and gallantry of it,
his fingers making their male slide up the
tulip-cleft in one of the shoved-up
legs of her shorts, she twists to
and from him until he is forced

to kiss and tickle her up,
to lead her to bed,

to lead her to this: she is
wearing a maternity smock
over the puckered shorts

tied with the drawstring,
she is barefoot, she is ironing one of the
husband's shirts, the iron nosing its way to a

stitched armpit, steaming and hooting
its way into the wrinkled cove of a pocket.

And how
does it smell?

Oh, sweet! Sweeter than anything!
Like those pouches on lupin flowers that smell

like pepper, like laundry
you've just pulled down off the line,

the peppery smell of wildflowers
along with the salt of laundered
perspiration

rising up with the steam.
But now it's a year later, now the
baby has come out into the world,
now it's time for the wife to

tuck her fed bee in his cradle,
but first she must carry him
to the window

to say hello to the fogged sunrise,
to hear the rusted cry of the big birds
of dawn (too tropical by half for the
concrete towers of Toronto), to be

jogged to the view of the whole city
sleeping, the upstairs screened-in
back sunporches still

all sagged and lost
in their hives of leaves
and sleep

Sometimes she feels scared
and humble thinking of the future, thinking
What if. What if something should happen
to her baby? What if she should fail him?
What if she's marked to become another statistic

(highway, divorce)

what if the husband
should become the dear departed?

Should depart into the afterlife?
Not the afterlife of the Victorian husband
(black crepe and sorrow) but being a
modern man in a windbreaker
and carrying his flight bag
out to his car

merely and terribly
into the afterlife of another life?
Someday — impossible to believe — all this
will be far behind her, this baby

lying in the incubated smell
of his own proud warm urine, his
tiny hands' delicate ownership of her breast,
the way he must see her, the welcoming

tumbled leer of the nipple.
But this morning she feels no pity
for that older woman (herself, turned old,
old as her own mother), this morning she feels
only her own power

(youth, cruelty)

here in this kitchen, holding this
sweet boy in her sun-warmed arms,

this morning she is Madam Abundance,
nothing can touch her

Elisabeth Harvor

The Difference

My son's penis disturbs me.
I wince when I see his open diaper
or his baby hand reach down and pull
the tiny sock of skin untouched by metal
where mine was split and bared
for cleanliness' sake and looking
like my Dad. It was the 50s when I was
born and everyone got cut,
but more than that, his penis says my own
is made around a wound, though still I cannot not
see the beauty I have spent so long to learn there;
once I read a poem by Sharon Olds who
saw in the rising head the kind of faith
and gentleness she observed as a child in the uprising
antennae of the garden slugs she used to watch, amazed,
and I wanted someone to see me that way,
emergent and trusting. I've read more poems since then.
I know the image is more than the eye's desire:
the erection she saw was unsheathing
itself from the folds it was born with, the way

nature protects its own, why the tongue,
despite its strength, hunkers down behind
a gate of polished stones, the heart keeps its fire inside
an ivory lantern, the tiny machinery of the ear
chirrups within the hollows of a scallop shell
deep beneath the poundage of the sea.
Keeghan, here is your body without artifact;
when you unfold yourself before another,
may you be seen not history first,
but with the beauty of my kind and
greater than my own.

Richard Harrison

A PRETTY SHAPE

I never stop listening to you sing
long enough to know what I think.
All I do is let it go on.

The bubble of song bounces towards me
over the wet surfaces of the kitchen
and you with your arms folded
in that tiny immemorial way you've observed,
your soft, small arms folded
over your chest where your breath
flows and unflows easily,
don't need to look at me.
The bubble of your song bounces towards me
its surface tension strong
as it shudders, recovers.
You let the song go where it wants.

When you've fallen asleep, or I think you've fallen
I withdraw, still singing
or perhaps still listening to you sing,
but you feel me going. Why am I going
always going, instead of listening to you sing?
Your hand knows better than mine

and with authority
of touch I cannot match
wraps me round you again.

Helen Dunmore

VIRGINA MAK *Untitled*

MY SON AT THE SEASHORE, AGE TWO

He laughs and a breeze
lifts his hair. His face tilts up
towards what has happened
to his hair, that it should lift,
and his laugh goes. Why
is this happening, his suddenly
serious face wants to know, and
what is happening. But
all it is is a little breeze
lifting his hair for a few seconds,
a little breeze passing by
on its way to oblivion —
as this day is on its way there too,
and as that day, twenty years ago,
was, too.

Don Coles

PRIMITIVE

Emma is learning to growl: a tremble primitive,
or machine; a below-language sound,
tiger outside the cave, pussycat in your ear,
lawnmower on the first suck of the gas.
Orbison (they begged and applauded him
do the growl, Roy). Sounds like she's working on
the big wet one says everything functions as it should:
good news, fossil pattern, apish grip,
vocabulary, *grrrrrr, grrrrrrr, grrrrrrrr.*

Richard Harrison

LOCOMOTION

Supported by my hands, Emma walks
the width of the park,
from kitchen to bedroom,
couch to door. She's quit talking: gone
are the multisyllables, the first word candidates.
All she does is *abababababa* —
and she walks. Right now the rest of
the alphabet is not important.
What she cares about
is getting from a to b.

Richard Harrison

FIRST BIRTHDAY

All night long we ate your cake for sustenance, the dog's
yellow eyes burning over you in the cabin, her long black body
a primitive vigilance. After you were born, the pale nurses
swept in like ghosts and ministered to you while the machines
kept count of your existence. You frightened us, deciding maybe
to turn back, and you went grey and washed out by daylight,
    hanging
in a nest of tubing like a hollow egg. I walked down into the old halls
with their windowless doors where the long-dead children
lingered, claimed by the things now simple to cure.
Then they released you to us and we swept you home, locked
the doors. Monstrous to prepare like that, for all of life
to unhand us suddenly, an actuarial moment, something drawn back
to reveal where we fit. But we evaded it; you lived, we spent
a summer morning decorating your first cake and at night danced
as though grief had never threatened us. Sugared from the day
    and safe
you slept beside the dog who knew how to carry live animals
in her mouth. She slipped like a dark oil into the night when we
    came in,

and lay in the grass and we lay near you and breathed your air
and by morning we'd all moved through each other, like blood.

Michael Redhill

Maureen Nolan *Bozena and Aaron*

HOLLIS STREET SQUARE, HALIFAX

Two kinds in the Saturday crowd:
first, the sharp-edged uneroded ones, single
or in fresh pairs, click by
briskly on assertive heels. Themselves
what they offer the world, a craft-fair of faces.

And then those with children at the ends
of their arms, small versions of themselves brightly
inflating as they drain down,
as though they'd opened a vein in their wrists and
out poured blood taking the shape of a child
pulling them by the hand:

those getting brighter and brisker and those
going invisible, sucked up the straws
of six-year-old arms, diving
inside small skins,
starting over again, small.

John Steffler

BEARHUG

Griffin calls to come and kiss him goodnight
I yell OK. Finish something I'm doing,
then something else, walk slowly round
the corner to my son's room.
He is standing arms outstretched
waiting for a bearhug. Grinning.

Why do I give my emotion an animal's name,
give it that dark squeeze of death?
This is the hug which collects
all his small bones and his warm neck against me.
The thin tough body under the pyjamas
locks to me like a magnet of blood.

How long was he standing there
like that, before I came?

Michael Ondaatje

Running Child

Watching my running child
On her seventh summer's beach
I see that other child
Incredulously allowed back
Through the afternoon's haze
To run beside her
Turning his head towards her
To gauge his joy

Thirty years ago

Don Coles

NIGHT TERROR

His cry of terror brings you,
tying yourself together and running
out of your dream to his dream
into the stunned, winter-ringing
air of his room, which the deep
hour has turned

into a malevolent den,
dead-of-night cosy,
your fear from your own
askew childhood tipped
into his childhood, the way
things he is used to could be
mockingly altered.

Cold sweat of delirium
might bead itself down the
gold stripes in the wallpaper
so that for a split second
before you turn on his lamp,
you are afraid to. When you do,
he raises an arm to ward off
the blow of the light.

His face the underside
of a small wing of fear
in the too-sudden brightness,
he turns it, collapsed,
to your nightgowned thigh.
You rub a small circle over
and over just behind his left ear

and remember how once
just after you got your hair
cut short and feathered,

he looked at you
with a narrowed distrust,
as if you might not be his real mother.

For a whole week he watched you.
Before he would eat his gingerbread men
he would break off their legs and sniff them,
and once you thought you saw him smell his milk
before he started to drink it, a dozen

cagey sips while he pretended not to be
spying on you as you packed carrot sticks
and apples into the small blue plastic trunk
he carries to school for his lunch break.

He's read his *Hansel and Gretel,*
he makes a wide berth around the oven
when you open its door to breathe in the perfect
comic-book heat of the gingerbread men. You've
planted caution so deep in his heart — a hardy, crabbed
perennial to keep him yours, keep him safe,
you know you've got no right to complain

when it turns into the gun
a redneck father might buy to protect
his family, the gun he hides under a filmy mound
of nightgowns yoked with bulletholes of smiling eyelet

in a drawer too high for a child to reach
unless he climbs to the top of a very tall stool,
the gun the tabloid baby climbs to, to brilliantly
find and aim at his mother.

From the moonlit, drugged kitchen
you bring him a cookie, a tall glass of water.
In absolute trust, he accepts first the glass,
hugging your thigh with one arm, leaning into it
as with one grateful, breath-desperate
swallow he drinks the water's long coldness
painfully down. Next, the cookie; but this he
eats in maddening slow-motion, a trick to
keep you near him while you are dying of exhaustion
and already, in your mind, giving your husband
his night moves: *move over, warm my feet, hold me.*

But not yet! This is a ceremony,
it must be carried out with child-pace precision:

with water, with wafer. Also, you are
the woman and he does not want you to go
too quickly back to that man, his father.

At long last he is willing to part with his glass,
another long-last and he is willing to raise his eyes
in night thanks, but then you see it, the old cunning

darkly flowering, the cunning he must have
decided is more manly than gratitude, the cunning
that might save him if ever he is stolen from you.

It's here, in this room, it's
out of its cage, it's alive, unspoken,
clear as a knell: How do I know *you* aren't
the bad person I saw in my dream?

Elisabeth Harvor

Noises Outside Your Window

You wake or fall asleep what does it matter
It is easy to pretend, to lift your eyes
at the last second, breathe slowly against
the cold of a mirror. Face your life
as though it were just noise outside your window.
A child is trapped in a well for two days
and news of that is beamed in thin strips of light
to anyone passing a humming tv set.
All of us afraid to turn away afraid
that the news is our lives.

When you wake your hands are empty but tired
as though they have held something tightly all night.
Your daughter coughs and you forget everything
that you have been sorting out in half wake logic.
You want to bring the morning to her in a kiss
Listen as she tells you the story of her toys
how they have fallen or are lost or are in love
with one another, as much drama as she can
imagine from her three years.

There is a spot in your brain that you can't control
that ignites when you are shopping or stuck in traffic
or listening to the radio. It is what you have inherited,
and passed on again your body agent to unknown phantoms.
That part of your brain does not sleep but projects dreams
for you all night. Your daughter stands
so powerful at the top
of the stairs her terror short-lived
lost in the cradle of your hug.
The halls in your house are narrow
ceilings so high they are nearly out of sight.
In it you sometimes feel like a seed about
to burst open. Clinging to the air it is still
possible to drown. What saves you is
your daughter's anxious cries her sleep as restless
as yours. Dreams invaded by the subtle
pressure of the room's air. In the morning
seeing the last lights fade in the city,
you know the power too, know the consequences
of holding your breath all night.

Robert Hilles

CHRISTINE MACK *"Mother o'mine, O mother o'mine"*

The little boy's hand, his hand full of trust,
trustingly offered to the bigger boy
as, without looking back, he walked away
from his mother to be beaten to death. Almost
more than I could bear, seeing in that slight back
turned forever, leaving forever, yours
as you walk off innocently towards
some horror I will fail to expect
or, worse, anticipate but not forestall.
Whenever I'm not holding you I know
nothing's *childproof:* no house, school, shopping mall,
no car, no bicycle. Nowhere to go
on God's green earth where children cannot fall
from mothers' arms. No. Nowhere to go.

Susan Glickman

My Son is Learning to Invent

My son is learning to invent
himself. Today he tells me of a time
I took him to a hospital and left him
alone there. He describes how he shook the steel
bars of his crib and cried as I left the room
without looking back.

(He was three. He had pneumonia
and I was alone. For a week,
I slept in a chair by his bed.
I only left once to buy him a book
when he was asleep.
The child in the next bed
had tubes in her throat and no-one
came to visit her at all.)

My son holds up his hands. If he could,
he would show me the desperate
welts the crib bars left and the black
square of my back cutting the light
from his eyes.

But I shake my head.

Stalemate.

Sometimes I show him pictures of myself
when I was his age. There is one
where I sit with my kid brother
in the middle of my grandfather's garden.
This is the one my son likes best.
But he insists that the boy,
my brother, who is fat and freckled,
is himself.

"Don't be ridiculous," I tell him,
"that's your Uncle Cam."

He tosses the photograph aside
and refuses to lose himself
in family history. What good is it
to him? Like that stupid riddle
about the sound of a tree falling
alone in a forest of trees.
The sun that shines over
these other children's heads
might as well be shining over
an empty pasture for all he cares.

In the top right corner of the photograph
is the cornfield where the children played
hide-and-go-seek.
We are still there, of course,
only now it is my son and I
who stalk each other
through the thin, green
leaves that bristle our bare arms
and whisper as they fold behind us, dry
secrets only they understand.

Whose childhood is this, anyway?

When we play in the park, he rides
in a swing so high above my head
the peak of his cap is a dark arrow
aimed at the heart of the sun.

"Look!" he calls.

And he lets go.

Only his body sinks through the abrupt
air towards concrete and the horrible
sound my throat can't make.

When the rest of the park
begins to move again
he is sprawled on his stomach
in the grass beyond the swing.

He gets to his feet
and his face is the colour of milk,
his lips sucked in
like an old man's.

I open my mouth, as he looks
up at me, wiping his palms on his jeans.
"Were you scared?" he asks.

My son is learning.

Bronwen Wallace

PAMELA HARRIS   *Yvel Mazerolle and Julien*

GIFTS

Right now, my son is crying
because the T-shirt he bought me for my birthday
is a bit too small.
He has flung himself on his bed
and his sobs carry him out
and further away from me,
the sound of them sinking
into the noise of the party downstairs
like the stubborn intervals
that try to force a song apart.

As for the shirt, it's not that small
and I'd wear it anyway,
because of the Mickey Mouse decal
he's had put on and my name, too,
because he saved up for it
because I'm his mother
and he's my child, all that corny truth
that would have been enough
even a year ago
and isn't now.
He can see for himself how it wrinkles
under the armpits and clings

to my shoulder-blades.
He can see it's not my style,
just as he knows he can't exchange it.
Can't take it back   can't take it back;
it's the chill of that,
laying its damp yellow touch
on the fine brown arm of his love
for years to come,
like the words we let fly
in the midst of an argument,
how they natter, dry birds,
in some empty room of the brain.

It seems all summer I have watched
this growing in him, seen it rise,
unbidden as that gesture he has for impatience,
my own, made with his father's hands.
Seen it glistening like oil on his skin
as he measures himself for the world,
studying how the older boys
dive from the raft at the cottage
and then, alone, practising all morning
just as his dad might concentrate
on the tongue and groove of a shelf, the slide
of a desk drawer, a perfect fit.

But when the big boys
rocked the raft until it flipped,
a huge thing, coming down
in a crash of water, shouts
from the beach, I saw him
in the shallows with the younger kids,
small against that spinning instant
when you'd have to jump free
or get your head bashed in
(how you'd have to be sure
you could, sure
as you could be)
saw the grey pinch of his cheeks
as he entered this knowledge
the way he'd enter
any other element, that first breath
that took him from me
stinging his lungs,

or when, as now
he returns for a while
from wherever his crying took him,
grinning up at me in this crazy shirt,
the cost of it already pinned to his chest

an old badge, so that soon
we will return together to the party
which is for my birthday, the day
when we begin to learn all this,
taking a lifetime just to recognize ourselves
and one day
from that whole terrible journey
to celebrate it.

Bronwen Wallace

At Three or Four or Five am

the green plastic of the respirator mask, my face watching
the green plastic of the mask hold your small breath,
drawn and released, your sleeping face calm
through the crib bars, against the crib bars,
my face watching your small battle gear,
your plastic breath travel the clear hose to the air compressor,
your extra lung, my steel help, steel hope,
clear plastic hope when your choking, your sure death
jerks me to the realistic kitchen,
the ritual medication, the refrigerator's pure light,
watching for your choking, your sure death
as my automatic fingers prepare the glass vial,
the chilled bronchodilator I believe in.
I believe in modern science,
the glass vial, the dial of my watch
counting the ten to twelve minutes of your miracle,
my salvation, the ten to twelve minutes
I grip your sleeping face calm against the crib bars,
grip the names of your sleeping features —
cheeks, eyes, nose, mouth — features of my salvation,
drawn and released, the names of my mother, my father,

the gods, name of my solitary childhood self, the child
alone in the strict hospital room, without mother, father,
the gods, child alone with each *acute exacerbation,*
alone with the ritual hope, ritual fear, pure motherless light.

Rhea Tregebov

MARRIED TO IT

The light does not reach the sink in front of you
as you do the dishes and think of your mother
all those nights alone washing dishes
trying to guess the meaning of things.
Her face was a glowing oval in the window.
Her eyes hidden. The earth trying to form
night in her mouth.

Soon you will go out and look
at the stars with your daughter and
see with her how each star is
fixed in space like we are fixed
inside moving only our bodies as we walk.
The earth, married to us, follows and we
feel in control of the whole damn thing.
You want to take your daughter to the place
where stooping you discovered the fullness of
blueberries their delicate skin bruised
in the picking. The blueberry hills are
covered with houses and roads now
and the only plants your daughter would find
are weeds you can no longer even name.

Your daughter kicks at your leg and you
turn to her expecting to see her smiling
but she is looking again at the stars
and holding her hat gingerly on her head.
As she speaks you know that in your mind
somewhere you are still picking blueberries
tasting your mother's pie listening
as a man plays a guitar and does not look
at you. Watching your daughter, you think
you can hear her heart forming a shape
she has learned from stars.
She stands now catching the moonlight
in her wide open mouth.

Robert Hilles

Pasta, or, Sometimes Food is Not a Toy

Kids' food is cute but cloying, much like children themselves, though we must not say so. Kids' food comes in funny shapes, bears, goldfish, dinosaurs, alphabets; it is bland and sweet and easy to digest, it pretends it is not food just a game, though we must not say so. How much pasta can anyone eat? A lot, apparently. Kids would not be happy reading an obscure French novel with a glass of good Bordeaux; they want the same story every night, wearing the same pyjamas, eating the same cookies with their milk, their milk in the same damn cup.

The pyjamas are in the wash, the book is shredded, Mommy's shredded too. Mommy would like to sit here for just one little moment and drink her damn wine (though she must not say so). But they know anyway; they come with sticky kisses and insistent hugs to tell Mommy how much they love her. *"Why was the spaghetti-maker so smart? She used her noodle." "Why was the spaghetti always late? It was living in the pasta!"* They come needing reassurance that Mommy

is not withdrawing her attention forever; that they
will not disappear if Mommy goes into another room.
Oh no, my darlings, you will not disappear. It is I,
it is I who am living in the pasta.

Susan Glickman

NURSERY, 11:00 PM

Asleep, the two of you,
daughter and son, in separate cribs,
what does it matter to you
that I stand watching you now,
I, the mother who did not smile all day,
who yelled Go away, get out, leave me alone
when the soup-pot tipped over on the stove,
the mother who burned the muffins
and hustled bedtime, tight-lipped.
You are far away,
beyond reach of whispered
amends. Yet your calm
breathing seems to forgive,
unwinding
into the air to mesh
like lace, knitting together
the holes in the dark.
It makes of this dark
one whole covering
to shawl around me.

How warm it is, I think,
how much softer
than my deserving.

Robyn Sarah

THE EXTRAVAGANT

Even the memory shames me and
it has happened more than once, my desperate
confusion nights when my son and I both have had far
too little sleep and morning finds me beside myself;
some wicked shouting thing, scared
and terrifying, stands beside my real,
good self and over him, a woman possessed
by the usual (fear). Thinking *he'll get sick* by which
I mean *this is not the life I want.*
I get my body confused with his.
I get my body confused with his
when I can't keep him safe, the way
I used to, when he was
my body. I get my body
confused with his, and it's
wrong and it hurts him,
I don't know how much.

  I imagine him, my son,
fifteen or twenty years from now,
a tolerant adult, forgiving me,
reading this and understanding,
like all the young, only

the extravagant, the outrageous claims
of motherhood, their oppressiveness and his own
imperative to escape them. Me.
Like all young men. No one will ever
be a part of his body.
   I think of the daughter I might have had,
will never have. So many holes in the universe.
Like the time at the farmhouse we looked up at the sky
and felt night fall off the mountain,
the hundreds of stars spilling out, lost
like the absences in our lonely bodies.
Or me shouting that morning in the beautiful hotel room
It costs too much!

Rhea Tregebov

WOLF AT THE DOOR

Jesse runs into the kitchen, finds me blue
over the morning news. "What happened to that man, Mama?"
A photo mostly boots, swinging in the breeze; head
slumped like a sunflower in autumn.
And my son, plump and smooth as autumn fruit,
clambers up my chair, smooshes his face against me. His arms
circle my neck a little too tightly as always; as always
not quite sure where his body ends
and mine begins.

"He's dead, Darling. His neck got caught in a rope
and he couldn't breathe." How far from the truth can I fly
now that he's five? Death he's already met,
lonely for his Grandpa who will never go fishing again,
but evil is still shadowy — the monster under the bed,
not the wolf at the door.

We study the picture together. "I'm careful, aren't I Mom?"
My sweet serious boy
whose limbs are dappled with bruises; lump on his noggin
the size and shape of a plum.
And who *is* careful, for all that.

I kiss his purple forehead, speechless
as so often these days.
My father is dead, and there's no one to protect me either.

Susan Glickman

APRIL HICKOX   *Untitled*

SUPPOSE

We're supposed to float together on a witchy cloud
over Toronto. Bake cookies, chocolate sprinkles
silver coins; take trips up and down elevators;
find the exact velvet dress you want
and you are supposed to let me buy it,
come home hugging it as though it were me.
We're supposed to run from room to room
in the Royal Ontario Museum naming birds,
find eggs, feathers, gummy nests
in drawers just at your height and you're
supposed to let me keep up but not get ahead.
We're supposed to eat ice cream at Greg's
watching ourselves in the mirror, watching
our tongues, supposed to take your
ever so much younger brother for a walk and you
get the apples because it's your job and you don't
trust me to remember.
We're supposed to play a game in which you tell me
I'm dead and I die for you flat out on the couch,
waiting to be resurrected, by you, but you don't.
You're supposed to, but you don't.

You have me lie there while your brother, anxious
shakes my knees. You turn away indifferent
towards the house you're building, me
waiting for you to bring me back say —
I don't want to be dead any more
and you're supposed to want me back, but you don't.
You're supposed to be seven now.
Supposed to be alive.
We're supposed to do something.
I don't know what, but we don't.

Ronna Bloom

BLACKBERRIES

Naomi with a full pail fell:
a tangle in the bramble looped
her ankle round, and caught it
like a hand, to pull her down
into the grassy gully, where she found
herself upon her back, the pail aloft
and upright, held secure against her chest.
Scarcely a berry spilled
of the precious catch! And so she lay
among the leaves, and laughed.

Bandanna girl, gatherer,
ditch-leaper, rock-scrambler,
bringer of bounty, may you always
find plenty, and safely
come home.

Robyn Sarah

STEP

At six, fairy tales are gospel.
The stepmother is black-eyed,
outlined in black. She's bloody-
minded and poodle-dressed.
She lives in the steady gaze
you give me, working to expose
the old hag in the young woman.
You spurn my goodnight kiss
and refuse to call me family,
but I know something you don't.
You make up the rules, kid,
when you strut into Thursday wearing
your brother's whistle cowboy hat
and bury my arms in the sand,
the impression of your hands left
like an embrace, the step between us
leapt over, the cold stream of it running
through me, through you, its own bond
shouted in a silent, stray hug

and volunteered in your copy-cat pose.
I won't say I love you until
these words cast no black magic.

Valerie Stetson

IN JUAREZ

This is the girl's first nightclub, in Juarez.
Kids can get in anywhere in border
towns, the trinketed streets and make-you-sick water.
Wide-hat musicians blare "La Cucaracha."
The father buys the girl a Shirley Temple and aims
his gin-soaked toothpick at an olive.

This afternoon they passed alleys alive
with rats and the souvenirs of Juarez,
hands slapping tortillas and hands held out for alms,
the gold cloth, a saint's knuckle stitched in its border
where anyone can kiss it, cockroaches,
bandits, and do the local people drink the water?

Fault of the Pope. That's what her
father says. The band cranks it up for the live
floor show, sequins and shimmying brooches.
The marquee said "Bestest dancers de Juarez!"
a fraction the price of shows across the border,
and look! — one is the girl's double, there, by the potted palms.

Rhinestones river her look-alike arms.
Her hairdo is the very same ducktail, slicked with water.
Same smile, eyes, colour. (Everyone is brown this side of the border.)
If the girl learned Spanish could she live
here? Would she fit right in, in Juarez,
ignoring for the moment the roaches?

She stares and wonders. The music reaches
its climax — maracas, a windmill of arms.
The father, who looks a little like the hero Benito Juarez,
holds his hand up to call the waiter.
The twin's bare back cha-chas towards the rest of her life.
In childish Spanish, the father gives his order.

A dried-up riverbed patrols the border.
Rifles and chainlink, uncountable breaches.
Are there, then, a number of possible lives?
Holes in the expected, like magic charms?
Whisha-whish go the dusty palms. *Answers are water.*
The girl sips the night-sugar taste of Juarez.

Dinner arrives on the arms of the waiter.
The father reaches for his *cabrito,* specialty of Juarez.
Life, whispers the sweating glass at the drink's sweet border.

Sue Wheeler

ELEGY FOR THE SPARROW

What's the point, the sullen boy asks,
of learning their names? *Bird*
should do. The indistinct grey of wings
against concrete, droppings on the faded fence.
And in spring, a racket at dawn, nuisance
of yellow gum, smashed eggshell, white
or blue, on the hard-hearted pavement. And he's sullen
for a reason. The city hard this winter,
with its tests and arguments; its losses.
His mother in one house, father in another.
And now it's spring. So what. Birds,
and their names, and the guide
so sure it's important. Like an ache,
this arch of branch over his head, glint
of light on the water. Something moves
in the space between words. Streak of smeared white
on his left and a call. Gull.
He knows that one.
Dun, dumb gull, gullible;
gull diving for nothing, for his fake toss
off the ferry. The island phoney too,
little stretch of green at the city's edge,
its quiet, the lift of the leaves

against the wind. But the city's still there,
ten minutes across the harbour.
And this blue — but the water's trash too:
pop cans and plastic bags, gasoline slicks,
little spills like the eyes in peacock feathers.
Peacock names itself, but the others?
As if you could know them
by their names: house from song
sparrow, the black or the greyish streaks,
reddish tail or chestnut bar through the eyes.
Know them with your eyes closed:
three sweet notes, then a lower note, then
a trill; or chirp, cheep, and various twitters.
Song. House. Do they belong to him now, the way he
belongs to his mother, father, the way his parents belong
to him? As if words belonged to the things they name.
Things named for colour, the lilac lilac,
orange orange. What will the world give him
if he knows its names? House. Song. The word *snake*
leaping to his mouth at the striped ribbon at his feet,
its green slip through the grass.

Rhea Tregebov

THESE PHOTOS OF THE CHILDREN
for Heidi

Twenty years have gone by since we took
these photos of the children, all three
together on a beach. They look up
from their beach which flows endlessly

towards you out of the front of every shot —
you can see that only a few footprints mar
the early-morning sand, and although you cannot
hear them you know that the cries of gulls are

here too, have only been intercepted by
the photos' glossy surface. Based on all
the evidence, this pancake-flat lake and cyclorama
of blue sky, it's going to be a hot day. How small

they look, we say, and along with time's preposterous
gulf comes a minute of relief, thinking how much
safer they are now, being grown —
because there were always such

fears when they were little! Fears that (hard to
remember what) all of them would just stray
off-screen we suppose, or sicken inscrutably,
or be hurried into a car one day

before we'd even noticed the idling,
and then gone, we'd be without
them forever. All of which, even though
you don't ask, has in fact come about —

look, we *have* lost them! — the three slender
swimsuited figures so steadfastly
standing here ducked out of sight
long ago, and will certainly

never be back. Taking
with them when they went the last
of the little summer dramas they used to
keep us entertained with on our fast-

tracking through the middle of our lives,
ad hoc scenes such as the recurrent, every
summer at least twice, heaping of sand dams
across the shallow stream you can see

silvering just behind them there. How
many mornings, July after July, we
laboured on these! And how seldom,
since then, has anybody

anywhere joined us half so willingly in
our lives' unimportant plans and plots
as they did, or listened half as hard to
our timeless advice, lots

of wise-person-on-mountain-top wisdom
about whatever-it-was — in this case
how, no matter how fast you heap up
the sand, all in one place

or swiftly in from both sides, it'll
never stop the stream on its own,
if this thing's to work you're going to
need the kind of stone

or stones that will sit up against the flow and
not just roll away, see? therefore, the flatter
on at least one side the better, see? *O, I see.*
All right. And although it doesn't matter

where you walk *below* the dam, when
you're above it try to move around without
too much splashing, OK? *OK I'll try.* No, that sort of
listening, so world-cancelling, went out

of fashion around here when the last dam went down,
and will never be back. Same with the rest of the lilliput stuff,
the little bent rakes and shovels, the unbent because
barely used sieves, more than enough

sand-moulds and mini-pails because that's what
the weekend guests usually brought —
there was even one left-in-the-rain ark with
pairs of everything, plus a lot

of random and chipped and limbless
and generally not really useful muss —
somebody treasured these things once, but
nobody does now, unless it's us.

So what's to learn here? Only how short a time
these three small ones chose to stay
around? Only how flat the lake was when it
halted for a second there? Only how hot the day

felt, how wide and long the impersonal sand
looked? That cloudless day, and brooding under
it, vast Time — what a marshalling of hosts against
three little hurrying-past ones! No wonder,

after such phalanxes, such serried
burnishings and dreadfully nodding plumes,
none of them's left! So yes, answering
the question, probably this *is*

all we've learned — which doesn't mean we don't
glimpse interestingly, now and then, in the rhyme
of our sleep, these three inflexible ones
behind their glossy torrent of clear time —

through which, if the dream will harden
and if both of us go on trying,
one day surely we'll drift towards these words
you're watching: day will start, a gull's first crying,

and then the dream will permit that sage advice, quick
nods, a young assenting voice that still condones
whatever's said or done to stem the rising stream and show
the sand, the caution above the dam, the flatly pleasing stones.

Don Coles

FAST CARS

for John and Lindy Stevenson

I liked how you arrived
for dinner last night, your arms
full of roots and cuttings for my garden,
how the music I was playing brought out
some crazy incident from your high-school days
so that soon we were all telling: first, those parts
we think we're old enough to laugh at now
and later, all that other stuff,
what Flannery O'Connor was getting at
when she said that "anybody who has survived his childhood
has enough information about life
to last him the rest of his days."
(How she should know,
her own life narrowed
to the distance she could cover
on crutches, on the farm
where her mother cared for her
and her stories grew, grace
like the brilliant turquoise of her peacocks,
widening before our eyes.)

I don't know how long
we sat that night. On the back porch
the plants leaned out through the dark
to the next day, the earth I'd turned
ready for them. But I know it was late
when we reached our own children,
all of them eager
to head off into whatever we fear
will take them furthest from us.
Booze or secrets. Sex. Fast cars.
How these things worry us, even as we know
that theirs may be the last generation
of kids on earth, our hearts contracting,
as they must, to what they think
they can comprehend.

After you'd left, I thought of a story
I hadn't told and how it fit with one I had:
when I was twelve, my best friend's brother Roger,
sixteen and drunk, went through the windshield
of his friend's Volkswagen two days before Christmas.
Six months later, the presents were still there,
unopened, on their hall shelf, and for years

my dad went on and on about German cars,
how dangerous they were,
another rant I had to tune out
with the rest of his war stories.
But if Freud's right about anything,
then it wasn't an accident
my first boyfriend drove one. Yellow.
That was the boy I told you about.
Doug, of the green eyes, who took me to a beach
that smelled of lemons for no reason at all,
the boy who taught me to drive the twisty road
to the highway, both of us pissed to the gills
all that summer when I got neither killed
nor pregnant and my father didn't know.
Didn't know as he glared from the doorway
every evening when Doug picked me up
and we drove off laughing.

And that's where we left him last night.

It's only remembering that other car, that
other child, that I can turn to find my father
smaller now, his thin shoulders rounded
as if to protect his chest and the knowledge
he has to keep there, as we all do,

for himself. Me, just driving into it then.
And him, just letting me go.

No. I should have said
having to.

Bronwen Wallace

Acknowledgements

Margaret Atwood, "You Begin," from *Two Headed Poems*, Oxford University Press (Toronto: 1978). Copyright © Margaret Atwood. Reprinted by permission of Oxford University Press.

Ronna Bloom, "Suppose," from *Fear of The Ride*, Harbinger Poetry Series/Carleton University Press (Ottawa: 1996); reprinted McGill-Queen's University Press (Montreal: 1999). Copyright © Ronna Bloom. Reprinted by permission of the author.

Don Coles, "My Son at the Seashore, Age Two," from *Forests of the Medieval World*, The Porcupine's Quill (Erin, Ontario: 1993); "Running Child," from *Landslides: Selected Poems*, McClelland & Stewart (Toronto: 1986); "These Photos of the Children," from *Kurgan*, The Porcupine's Quill (Erin, Ontario: 2000). Copyright © Don Coles. Reprinted by permission of The Porcupine's Quill.

Helen Dunmore, "A Pretty Shape," from *Out of the Blue: Poems 1975-2001*, Bloodaxe Books (Tarset, UK: 2001). Copyright © Helen Dunmore. Reprinted by permission of Bloodaxe Books.

CONTRIBUTORS' NOTES

Margaret Atwood's poetry, like her fiction, is known and acclaimed around the world. She has had eleven volumes of poetry published in Canada, the United States and the United Kingdom, as well as in fifteen other countries. Her most recent novel, *The Blind Assassin*, won the Booker Prize.

Ronna Bloom's first book of poetry, *Fear of the Ride*, was nominated for the Gerald Lampert Memorial Award. Her second, *Personal Effects*, was published in 2000. She lives in Toronto.

Don Coles is one of Canada's most accomplished poets. He has published ten collections of poetry, including *Forests of the Medieval World*, which won the Governor General's Award and *Kurgan*, which won the Trillium Prize for 2001. For ten years he was Senior Poetry Editor at the Banff Centre for the Arts. Until his recent retirement, he taught creative writing at York University.

Helen Dunmore's poetry, children's writing and fiction is acclaimed both in her native England and internationally. Her third novel, *A Spell of Winter*, won the Orange Prize; she has since published three further novels and two collections of short stories. She was born in Yorkshire and now lives in Bristol.

Susan Glickman is the author of four books of poetry, most recently *Hide & Seek*. She has also written the award-winning work of literary criticism, *The Picturesque & the Sublime: A Poetics of the Canadian Landscape*. She and her husband, glass artist Toan Klein, have two children.

Big Breath of a Wish is **Richard Harrison**'s fourth book of poetry. He teaches English and Creative Writing at Mount Royal College in Calgary, where he lives with his wife, Lisa Rouleau, their daughter Emma and their son Keeghan.

Elisabeth Harvor's first volume of poetry, *Fortress of Chairs*, won the Gerald Lampert Memorial Award. Her third collection of short stories, *Let Me Be the One,* was short-listed for the Governor General's Award. Her first novel, *Excessive Joy Injures the Heart*, was released in 2000.

Robert Hilles lives in Calgary with his partner Pearl Luke. His most recent book of poetry, *Higher Ground*, was published in 2001. *Cantos for a Small Room* won the 1994 Governor General's Award for poetry. His first book of prose, *Raising of Voices*, won the 1994 Writers' Guild of Alberta Georges Bugnet Award for best novel. He recently finished his second novel, *A Gradual Ruin*, and is at work on a third.

Ken Howe played principal horn in the Regina Symphony for eight years. In 2000, he was the recipient of the City of Regina Writing

Award. The manuscript for his first book of poetry, *Household Hints for the End of Time*, received a John V. Hicks Manuscript Award in 2000; the book received the Saskatchewan Book Award in 2001.

Michael Ondaatje's most recent book of poetry is *Handwriting*. His other books include *Running in the Family, Coming Through Slaughter, The Cinnamon Peeler* and the internationally celebrated novels *In the Skin of a Lion, The English Patient* and *Anil's Ghost*. He was born in Sri Lanka and came to Canada in 1962. He lives in Toronto.

P.K. Page is the author of over a dozen books of poetry, fiction and non-fiction, and has been honoured with numerous awards, including the Governor General's Award for poetry. Her paintings have been exhibited internationally. Having travelled widely for much of her life, she now makes her home in Victoria, British Columbia.

Michael Redhill is a poet, playwright, novelist, and an editor with *Brick: A Literary Journal*. His novel, *Martin Sloane*, was short-listed for the Giller Prize. He lives in Toronto with his family.

Robyn Sarah was born in New York City to Canadian parents and has lived most of her life in Montreal. She studied philosophy at McGill University and music at the Conservatoire du

Québec. She is the author of several poetry collections as well as two collections of short stories.

The author of four books of poetry and a novel, **John Steffler** lives in Corner Brook, Newfoundland. His next book of poems, a new and selected poems titled *Helix,* will be published by Véhicule Press in 2002. He is currently Writer-in-Residence at the University of New Brunswick, where he is working on a new novel.

Valerie Stetson received the 2001 Bronwen Wallace Award for short fiction. Her fiction and poetry have appeared in *The Dalhousie Review, Canadian Literature, Room of One's Own, Fireweed* and *The Globe and Mail.* She lives in Kelowna, BC, and is currently working on a collection of short fiction.

Rhea Tregebov has published five collections of poetry, most recently *The Strength of Materials.* In addition to her poetry, Tregebov has edited numerous anthologies, and has also written five popular children's picture books.

Bronwen Wallace was the author of five acclaimed collections of poetry, including the posthumous *Keep That Candle Burning Bright.* Her collection of short stories, *People You'd Trust Your Life To,* a national bestseller, is about to be reissued. Her writing has been honoured with the National Magazine Award, the Pat Lowther Award and the Du Maurier Award for Poetry, as well as the Commonwealth Poetry Prize. Wallace died in 1989.

Sue Wheeler's first book of poetry, *Solstice on the Anacortes Ferry,* won the Kalamalka New Writer's Prize and was short-listed for both the Pat Lowther and the Gerald Lampert Memorial Awards. *Slow-Moving Target,* her second collection of poetry, was short-listed for the Pat Lowther Memorial Award and the Dorothy Livesay Prize.

David Zieroth's sixth book of poems is *Crows Do Not Have Retirement.* He won the Dorothy Livesay Prize for his fifth book, *How I Joined Humanity at Last.* His poems have been nominated for the National Magazine Award and have appeared in more than thirty-five anthologies.